Learning to Read Music

Learning to Read Music

BY ROBERT LILIENFELD

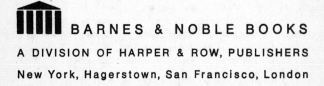

BARNES & NOBLE BOOKS
A DIVISION OF HARPER & ROW, PUBLISHERS
New York, Hagerstown, San Francisco, London

A hardcover edition of this book was originally published by Funk & Wagnalls Company.

First BARNES & NOBLE BOOKS edition published 1979.

ISBN: 0-06-463495-7

87 88 89 90   10 9 8

TO
KATHRYN, HUGO, AND ADAM—
a right jolly crew

Contents

PART ONE

ELEMENTARY NOTATION
AND THEORY

PART TWO

CLASSROOM EXERCISES IN INTERVALS,
MELODY, AND RHYTHM

PART ONE
Elementary Notation
and Theory

Introduction

This book is intended to fulfill several purposes at once. First, it is designed as a self-teaching manual of the elements of music notation and music theory. It is certainly true that the beginner would do well to learn music under the guidance of a teacher, but there is a very large component of the musical ABC's which can be self-taught and, in fact, should be. The beginner can never tell by himself when he is singing off pitch or has missed the beat in a complicated rhythmic pattern. For this, guidance by a teacher is indispensable. But if the beginner will carefully work his way through the self-taught portion of this book, and will check his own intonation against a pitch-pipe or other instrument when singing the exercises, he will go a long way toward being able to follow a musical score when listening, if not toward being able to perform, as well as toward making his progress in practical work, whenever he undertakes it, as quickly as possible. The second purpose of this book is to serve as a textbook for classes in which the elements of music are taught. The first part is that material for which the student is responsible; since all exercises are worked (solutions are in an Appendix), the student can check his own progress. The second part of the book is a set of sight-reading and -singing exercises suitable for beginning groups.

The person who wishes to study by himself is advised to work his way through this book prior to taking a short course in music fundamentals like those offered in many adult-education centers and music schools throughout the country.

The book, in addition to serving as a text for a beginning class, also covers the fundamentals of music theory. This is offered because, in the early stages of learning music, it is impossible to tell where music theory leaves off and music notation begins, as, for example, with scales, keys, and key signatures. But only such theoretical material is included as is necessary for the practical purposes of reading and performing music, and for understanding some of the peculiarities of music notation.

The beginner will need only a few practical materials: a music-writing book and a pitch-pipe. Those working by themselves may also want a metronome for doing the exercises in rhythm and meter.

Some readers may wonder at the inclusion of materials on the Dorian, Phyrgian, and other modes, and on such matters as C-clefs, transposing instruments, and orchestral scores. This has been done because the author has discovered, in the course of his teaching, that his classes of adult beginners consist of three basically different groups, each having different interests:

(1) *Beginners who plan to study such instruments as the piano, violin, etc.*   These students may study and perform for years a repertory of pieces that require no knowledge of the modes, the C-clefs, or of transposing instruments.

(2) *Beginners interested in choral singing.*   These are amateurs who do not intend to master an instrument, or have once in the past studied an instrument, and want to return to musical activities. For this group, joining a chorus is an ideal means of music-making without long and arduous hours of prac-

ticing. But such beginners who do join a chorus are likely to be confronted with modal music, and even with editions of choral music that use C-clefs, quite early along in their careers. Since choral singing has grown immensely in popularity in recent years, the inclusion of some discussion of modes and C-clefs is quite justified.

(3) *Armchair music lovers.* Those who have no ambitions to perform, but who want to follow performances or recordings of their favorite compositions with the score in hand, are, as a rule, completely baffled by the anachronisms and peculiarities of orchestral scores. Enough explanatory material has been included to make an orchestral score more meaningful to the beginner.

SUGGESTIONS FOR CLASSROOM USE

Many points throughout the text can be illustrated at the keyboard by the instructor, or by his having the class sing a simple illustrative melody, or tap a rhythmic pattern. These are indicated at appropriate points in the text. In addition, the section *Classroom Exercises* constitutes a complete course in graded exercises, sufficient for a full semester.

The material in this book is a result of the author's experience in teaching beginner's classes in music at the New School for Social Research over the past five years. It has thus been tested and re-tested under practical conditions of use. If a class is sufficiently large, it may be profitably divided for the performance of two-part exercises; a group of eight or more is often sufficient for these, which form a valuable part of the beginner's experience in training the ear. Therefore, a full course of such exercises is also included.

Experience has convinced the author that one semester of solid work will supply the beginner with everything he needs to go on to any kind of further work in music; this book is designed to fulfill that purpose.

I

The Musical Staff

THE MUSICAL ALPHABET

There are only seven different basic tones in our musical system; these are named after the first seven letters of the alphabet: A, B, C, D, E, F, G. All other tones are either repetitions or alterations of these seven basic ones.

PITCH

Everyone is familiar with the difference between high tones and low ones. We experience sound as occurring in a tonal space, having the continuous dimension which we call high-to-low. This acoustical property (*pitch*) is reflected in musical notation: what is heard as high or low in tonal space is seen as correspondingly high or low in musical notation.

THE MUSICAL STAFF

Tonal space is symbolized by a series of lines and spaces:

Not only are the lines used; the spaces are used also. Although we may think of the entire range of tonal space as being traversed by this system of lines and spaces, in practice it is now customary to print only five lines. This is called *the musical staff*. At various times in the history of music, the staff has ranged from four lines up to ten or more, but a staff of five lines seems to be the most convenient and readable.

To speak more precisely, the staff consists of five lines and four spaces, giving a total of nine degrees of musical pitch within the limits of the staff. A note may be written on a line or in a space. The normal order of writing the notes of the musical alphabet in succession is: line-space-line-space, etc. Thus, if the first line of the staff (the lowest line) were the note A, the first space would be B, the second line would be C, and so on:

A   B   C   D   E   F   G   A   B   C

We note that once we reach the tone G, we simply start over again with the seven letters, for the succeeding tones: E, F, G, A, B, C, D, E, F, G, A . . . etc.

EXERCISE 1: Practice writing notes on lines and spaces, in order to become familiar with the staff, by copying the following sequence of notes.

EXERCISE 2: Following are some note sequences. Assuming that the first note shown has the letter name as indicated, write in the names of the succeeding notes. (Correct answers to all exercises are given in the Appendix.)

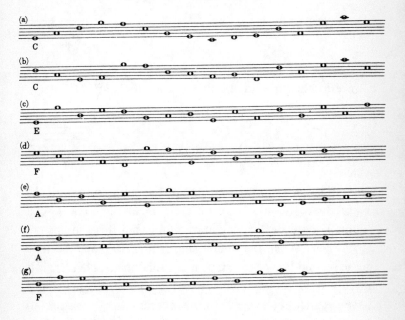

CLEF SIGNS

The staff by itself does not assign any letter name to any particular line or space. We have emphasized this in the exercises above by assigning different letter names to the lines and spaces. In order for the reader to know which letter names have been assigned to the lines and spaces, a special group of symbols are employed, called *clef signs*. There are several of them in common use, so that the musician is free to assign almost any letter to any line or space. The clef sign most familiar to beginners is the G-clef: 𝄞 . It is a stylization of the Gothic letter G: . This is a symbol which assigns the letter G to a particular degree of the staff; it is commonly used today to assign the letter G to the second line of the staff. Note that it does so in that it curls around the second line of the staff:

If it were to curl around the first line of the staff:

this would assign G to the first line of the staff, so that all the lines and spaces would have different meanings. The G-clef was actually used in this way at one time, but this use has become obsolete. When the G-clef sign is used to place the tone G on the second line of the staff, it is called the *treble clef;* it is commonly used for high voices and high instruments. Once we have assigned the letter G to the second line of the staff, all the other lines and spaces now have a determined letter value:

The Treble Clef

G   E   F   G   A   B   C   D   E   F   G

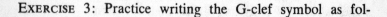

EXERCISE 3: Practice writing the G-clef symbol as fol-

lows: write the vertical stroke first ⎢, then add the small loop at the top ⸙ , followed by the large loop ⸘ , and finish by curling around the second line ⸙ . Practice writing at least half a dozen signs, until you can write them quickly and easily.

EXERCISE 4: Write the correct letter names for the notes of the treble clef shown below. Write the letter under each note.

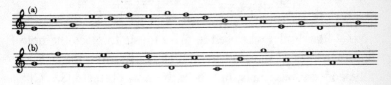

LEGER LINES

If a melody climbs above or below the staff, the system of lines and spaces is simply extended as needed:

In this way, we can think of tonal space as being traversed by lines and spaces throughout the full range of all tones; the staff simply materializes five of those lines for convenience. If more lines are needed, we materialize them as needed; these are the leger lines.

EXERCISE 5: Write the correct letter names for the notes shown below, and copy out the sequence of notes, writing the letter under each note.

THE BASS CLEF

The note G is not the only point of reference in music notation. The notes C and F are also used. The F-clef sign looks like this: 𝄢. It assigns the note F to the fourth line of the musical staff. When this clef sign is used, the staff is defined in a way different from that in effect when the G-clef is used. The lines and spaces of the staff are now defined as:

The Bass Clef

F　G　A　B　C　D　E　F　G　A　B

(Note: The F-clef was used in older music to place the note F on other lines of the staff as well as the fourth—the old baritone and sub-bass clefs, but those are now obsolete. See Chapter IX, on score reading.)

EXERCISE 6: Practice writing the bass-clef sign. Note that it consists of: the "head," which is placed on the fourth line; the curve; and the two dots like a full colon, which are placed in the third and fourth spaces of the staff. This clef sign is a stylization of the old Gothic F.

Writing the bass-clef sign:

1　2　3

EXERCISE 7: Write the correct letter names for the notes shown below.

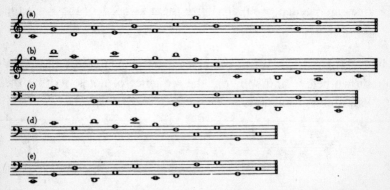

THE C-CLEF

A third way of defining the tones of the staff is by reference to the note C. The C-clef looks like this: 𝄡 . It too is derived by way of decoration from the letter C. This, like the other clef signs, can be placed on more than one line of the staff, but some of these usages are obsolete. However, two forms of the C-clef still survive in modern usage; anyone hoping to read an orchestral score must be acquainted with them. The first places the note C on the third line of the staff:

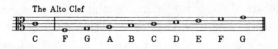

This is called the *alto clef;* it is used today by the viola.

The second form in current use is that which places the tone C on the fourth line of the staff:

This is called the *tenor clef*. It is sometimes used for the higher notes of the violoncello, the bassoon, and the trombone.

For practical purposes, the beginner need work only with the treble and bass clefs, and may add the alto clef later on.

EXERCISE 8-A: Write the correct letter names for the notes shown below. (Answers are given in the Appendix.)

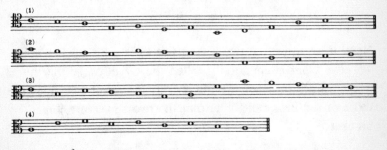

EXERCISE 8-B: Practice writing C-clef signs for the alto and tenor clefs, as shown below.

THE GREAT STAFF

There are three main reference points for music notation: F, C, and G. The tone C is called Middle C, as it lies about midway in the range of audible tones, and also is in about the middle of the piano keyboard. The tone G is the first G *above* Middle C, five steps above; the tone F is the first F *below* Middle C, five steps below it. We may picture the Great Staff as consisting of eleven lines, with the Middle C line the midmost:

In practice, only ten lines are shown, with the Middle C line left out:

Now, if we move the two sets of five lines a bit further apart, we have what is commonly called the *Great Staff;* the upper five lines are those of the treble clef; the lower five lines are those of the bass clef. Note that the two staves are joined by brackets:

The Great Staff

Note that tones can be written with reference to the treble clef, by using leger lines, which actually run low enough to be written on the bass clef:

Thus, the two melodies shown are identical. Similarly, a melody may be written with reference to the bass clef which runs high enough to be written in the treble clef; the two examples below are identical, note for note:

OCTAVE INDICATORS

There are various systems in use for designating exactly which octave is being referred to. None of these systems is universal. Perhaps the most widely used is the one below:

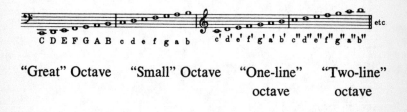

C D E F G A B   c d e f g a b   c' d' e' f' g' a' b'   c" d" e" f" g" a" b"

"Great" Octave   "Small" Octave   "One-line"   "Two-line"
octave   octave

The octave below the Great Octave is called the Contra Octave. Its letters are designated by subscripts: C_1, D_1, E_1, etc.

The octaves above the Two-Line octave are the "Three-line" (c''', d''', etc.), and the "Four-line" octaves.

MUSICAL STAVES AND SCORES

If a composition is written for just one instrument, the musical score will consist of a series of just one staff; but if it is written for more than one part, then the score will consist of as many staves as there are parts, bound together by brackets. Thus, a trio will look like this:

The person who reads the score does not read the first staff, then go back to the second staff, and so on. Rather, all three staves must be read simultaneously.

The simplest form of score is the piano score, which we have seen earlier; the treble staff is generally played by the right hand of the pianist; and the bass staff by the left. Note that the two staves are bound by a bracket; they are read simultaneously.

INTERVALS

SIMPLE INTERVALS

Any two tones sounding simultaneously or in succession form a musical *interval*. The musical intervals are simply named by counting the tones framed by the interval. Thus, the interval C to F covers four tones—C, D, E, F, and so is called a *fourth*. Note that we adopt the convention of counting from the first tone upward to the first tone that has the name. Thus, if we counted downward from C to F, the interval framed would not be the same—C, B, A, G, F covers five tones, and is called a *fifth*. The two tones C–D form a *second;* C–E form a *third;* C–A form a *sixth,* etc. In general, an interval is named simply by counting the tones; thus, the interval D–B covers six tones: D, E, F, G, A, B, and is therefore called a *sixth*. We will see from this that an interval is a definite musical entity in its own right. Thus, the fifth is a quite specific sound; it can be materialized by the tones C–G (C, D, E, F, G form a fifth), or by D–A, E–B, and so on. In one sense, it is quite valid to say that music does not consist of tones but rather of the intervals which the tones serve to materialize. A knowledge of intervals is therefore of basic importance.

THE OCTAVE

One of these intervals is unique, the octave. Every pair of tones framing eight notes are given the same name: C–D–E–F–G–A–B–C', and the same is true for D to D', E to E', and so on.* For this interval, the two tones blend into so close a unity that each appears to be a repetition of the other at a higher or lower level of pitch. The word octave, of course, means eight. All other intervals are framed by tones that are differently named; the octave is framed by tones having the same name; the octave is an identity.

Note: the prime sign ′ is here used simply to refer to a tone an octave higher than the same letter tone without the prime sign. Thus:

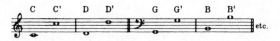

COMPOUND INTERVALS

In naming intervals that are wider than the octave, musicians follow two practices; the first is simply that of starting all over again; thus the two tones C–D', which frame nine tones: C–D–E–F–G–A–B–C'–D' may be called a *second;* or, one may simply count the full number of tones and call it a *ninth.* Both terms are used interchangeably. If the two tones C–D' are sounded simultaneously, they are commonly called a second, in that the second and the ninth are identical from the point of view of harmony; if they are sounded in succession, they are then called a ninth, inasmuch as there is a great difference in a melody between a second and the leap of a ninth.

We will adopt the convention of naming all intervals wider than the octave as though they occur within the frame of one octave. Thus, C–E', though literally a *tenth,* will be regarded as the same as a *third.*

EXERCISE 9-A: Write the following at the same pitch, in bass clef. Label each note.

EXERCISE 9-B: Write the following at the same pitch, in treble clef. Label each note.

EXERCISE 9-C: Write 9-A above in tenor clef at the same pitch. Label each note.

EXERCISE 9-D: Write 9-B above in alto clef at the same pitch. Label each note.

EXERCISE 9–E: Write the following an octave higher, in treble clef. Label each note.

EXERCISE 9-F: Write the following an octave lower, in bass clef. Label each note.

II

Duration of Notes

The most commonly used notes are:

(1) The Whole-Note   𝅝

(2) The Half-Note   𝅗𝅥   or   𝅗𝅥

(3) The Quarter-Note   𝅘𝅥   or   𝅘𝅥

(4) The Eighth-Note   𝅘𝅥𝅮   or   𝅘𝅥𝅮

(5) The Sixteenth-Note   𝅘𝅥𝅯   or   𝅘𝅥𝅯

(6) The Thirty-second Note   𝅘𝅥𝅰   or   𝅘𝅥𝅰

There are other note values: the double whole-note, also called the *breve:* 𝆺 and, following after the thirty-second note, the sixty-fourth note: 𝅘𝅥𝅱 . These are less commonly used.

Notes are constructed of two components: 1) The *note head,* which may be white or black; 2) the *stem,* which may be joined to the note head in either of two ways—it may be attached to the left of the note head, in which case it descends:

♩ , or it may be attached to the right of the note head, in which case it ascends: ♩ . *The meaning of a note is not affected by the attachment of the stems*. It is common practice when writing notes above the third line of the staff, to attach stems below the note head (to the left). When writing notes below the third line of the staff, the stems are normally written ascending, to the right of the note head.

THE RELATIVE VALUES OF THE NOTES

The whole-note lasts twice as long as does the half-note; the half-note lasts twice as long as the quarter-note; the quarter-note is twice the length of the eighth-note, and so on. Or, conversely, the half-note moves twice as fast as does the whole-note, the quarter-note twice as fast as the half-note, etc.

The basic principle of note division, then, is *binary*, in that each note is twice as long as its next shortest note, and half the value of the next longest.

DOTTED NOTES

If we wish to follow a *ternary* principle of note division, then dotted notes must be used. Addition of a dot to a note increases its duration by one half its original value. Thus, the quarter-note equals two eighth-notes; a dotted quarter-note equals three eighth-notes:

TERNARY DIVISION OF NOTES

Our notation system is really binary, and the only way to have ternary subdivisions on all rhythmic levels is by the make-shift device of writing "triplets," as follows:

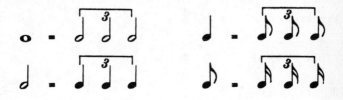

FLAGS AND BEAMS

Eighth-notes, sixteenth-notes, and notes of shorter duration may be written with flags attached to each stem; or, if these notes occur in groups, they may be connected together with beams, without changing the rhythmic meaning:

RESTS

Corresponding to each note with its specific duration are the rests, the silences of a specific duration. These are as follows:

Whole-note rest

Half-note rest

Quarter-note rest

Eighth-note rest

Sixteenth-note rest

Thirty-second-note rest

As before, the whole-note rest (or silence) is twice as long as a half-note rest, and so on.

Just as notes could be dotted, so can silences, in which case they assume the following values, the same as do their corresponding notes:

Dotted whole-note rest

Dotted half-note rest

Dotted quarter-note rest

Dotted eighth-note rest

DOUBLE DOTTED NOTES AND RESTS

The reader will also occasionally encounter notes followed by not one but two dots. The principle is that each dot adds to the note length one-half the value of the symbol immediately before it.

Thus:

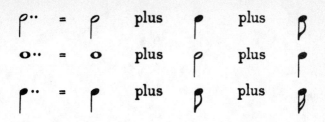

TIES

The duration of a sound can be extended in still another way. The following represents three quarter-notes in immediate succession:

If this were to be played on the piano, the performer would strike the key three times in succession. But if it were desired to change this into just one sound lasting three times as long, the notes could be linked together by ties:

The following are all identical in duration and sound:

The use of ties instead of dotted notes, or rather, along with them, makes possible sounds of a duration equal to any values the musician may want.

EXERCISE 10: Write each of the following notes in two different ways, by the use of ties:

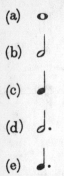

(a)

(b)

(c)

(d)

(e)

EXERCISE 11: Exercises in Note Values. Combine the paired melodies below by writing them in the same staff. Be sure to write those notes which sound simultaneously in vertical alignment, as in the example below. Distinguish the melodies by having the note stems of the higher melody go upward, and those of the lower melody downward.

Proceed by writing out one of the melodies first. It is important to allot more space to the longer note values, in order to avoid the crowding of shorter note values that correspond to them in the other melody.

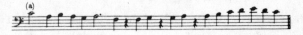

METERS AND TIME SIGNATURES

Musical compositions are normally divided into regular sections called *measures,* or *bars*.

The measures are demarcated by what are called bar-lines; the space between two bar-lines is called a measure, or a bar.

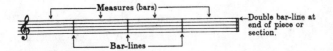

The human pulse is the standard measure of meter. If we imagine all music as unfolding over a series of steady, equal pulses, called *beats,* we are able to group these regular beats into measures. We may assign two beats to a measure, three beats, four beats, and so on. We may also arbitrarily assign any note value to be equal to the beat.

BINARY METERS

If music is written with two beats to the measure, the first beat is conventionally treated as strong, or accented; the second as weak, or unaccented. We are free to assign any note to the beat. Thus, we may have two whole-notes to the measure, two half-notes, two quarter-notes, two eighth-notes, etc.

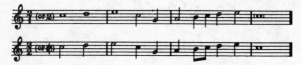

In the first example above, we have two whole-notes to the measure. This of course does not mean that there cannot be quarter-notes, half-notes, etc., in the measure, but rather that they must add up to no more and no less than two whole-notes. This meter is rarely used today.

Two-quarter and two-eighth meters are more common:

TERNARY METERS

This is a meter in which there are three beats to the measure. The first beat of the measure is strong, or accented; the second and third beats are weak, or unaccented. The ternary meters most commonly used are: three-half time, three-quarter time, three-eighth time, and three-sixteenth time. Three whole-notes to the measure are rarely used.

TIME SIGNATURES (1)

A time signature commonly appears as a fraction. For example, three-quarter time will be indicated by $\frac{3}{4}$. The numerator of the fraction tells us how many beats to the measure (3). The denominator tells us what type of note is made equal to the beat—in this case, the quarter-note. It may be helpful for the beginner to think of the time signature as 3 times $\frac{1}{4} = \frac{3}{4}$. Similarly, $\frac{3}{2}$ at the beginning of a composition means 3 times $\frac{1}{2} = \frac{3}{2}$, or, that there are three beats to the measure, and the half-note has the beat.

COMPOUND METERS

Four to the measure is sometimes regarded as a simple meter, sometimes as compound. We will consider it a simple meter. The first beat of each measure is regarded as a strong accent; the second and fourth beats are regarded as weak, or unaccented; the third beat is regarded as a secondary accent, not as strong as the first beat of the measure, but stronger than the second and fourth beats of the measure. Thus, a measure of four might be counted as:

> 1   2   3   4   1   2   3   4
>
> *strong*–and–weak–and–*strong*–and–weak–and– etc.

The beat may be assigned to any of the note values: whole- or half-notes, quarter-notes, eighth-notes, etc.

The true compound meters are as follows:

Six to the Measure   This is a compound binary meter, in

that every measure is considered to consist of two principal accents, each of which is divided into three subdivisions:

1   2   3   4   5   6

strong–weak–weak   *strong*–weak–weak

The time signatures may be: $\frac{6}{4}$, $\frac{6}{8}$, and $\frac{6}{16}$.

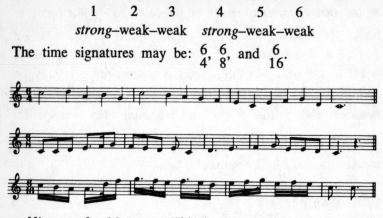

Nine to the Measure   This is a multiple of three; each measure has three main accents, each of which is divided into three equal subdivisions:

1   2   3   4   5   6   7   8   9

strong–weak–weak   *strong*–weak–weak   *strong*–weak–weak

Time signatures commonly used are: $\frac{9}{8}$, and $\frac{9}{16}$

Twelve to the Measure   This is a compound of four to the measure, in which each main beat is subdivided into three.

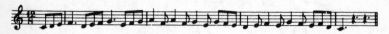

OTHER METERS

Composers will occasionally attempt meters of 5, 7, and other unusual combinations. These are difficult to sustain as

we tend to break such combinations down into the simpler, more basic meters. Thus, we tend to hear 5 as a combination of three plus two, or two plus three; 7 is heard as three plus four or four plus three. Where a composer intends a fairly consistent alternation of the number of beats to a measure, the time signature will be shown as a double signature, as follows:

The double signature simply means that there will be measures of three beats and measures of four.

TIME SIGNATURES (2)

We may now summarize the time signatures described above, and add some symbols commonly seen.

Binary Meters: $\frac{2}{1}$ (or 2); $\frac{2}{2}$ (or ¢); $\frac{2}{4}$; $\frac{2}{8}$

[Note that $\frac{2}{2}$ is more commonly indicated by the following symbol: ¢.]

Ternary meters: $\frac{3}{1}$ (or 3); $\frac{3}{2}$; $\frac{3}{4}$; $\frac{3}{8}$; $\frac{3}{16}$

Meters of Four: $\frac{4}{4}$ (or **c**); $\frac{4}{8}$; $\frac{4}{16}$

[Note that $\frac{4}{4}$ is more commonly indicated by the following symbol: **C**. These symbols are remnants of an older (medieval) system of rhythmic and metric notation.]

Meters of Six: $\frac{6}{4}$; $\frac{6}{8}$; $\frac{6}{16}$

Meters of Nine: $\frac{9}{8}$; $\frac{9}{16}$

Meters of Twelve: $\frac{12}{8}$; $\frac{12}{16}$

EXERCISES IN METRIC VALUES

EXERCISE 12-A: Rewrite the following melodies, doubling the note values (make quarter-notes into half-notes, etc.). Alter the time signatures appropriately.

EXERCISE 12-B: Rewrite the following melodies, halving the note values (make half-notes into quarter-notes, etc.). Alter the time signatures appropriately.

EXERCISE 12-C: Add bar-lines and time signatures to the following rhythmic patterns. Each exercise begins with a complete measure.

EXERCISE 12-D: For each of the following melodies, indicate the placement of the beats in each measure by writing the appropriate numeral over the note corresponding to that beat. Example below:

THE WRITING OF NOTES AND RESTS IN MEASURES

In order to keep the metric patterns clear at all times, it is a general principle of writing music that, wherever possible, each beat of the measure is to be marked by a rest or note, even if this means using more symbols than would at first glance appear necessary. Thus, in $\frac{6}{8}$ time, where the main (accented) beats are 1 and 4, a rhythmic pattern such as follows should be written:

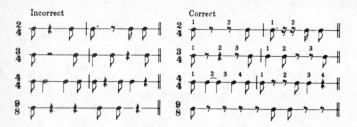

Although it could be written as below, this would be incorrect, since it is misleading as to the true meter:

We note that the time signature does not tell us only the number of beats to the measure; it also tells us where the accents are placed. Correct musical orthography tries to keep the placement of accents always clear to the reader. There are no strict rules for this, only a certain amount of common sense.

Below are some rhythmic and metric patterns, written to show both the correct and the incorrect ways of writing them. [Note: A whole-note rest is commonly used to indicate the rest of an entire measure, regardless of the time signature.]

EXERCISE 13-A: Complete each of the following measures by adding one note.

EXERCISE 13-B: Complete each of the following measures by adding one note and one rest.

EXERCISE 14-A: Combine each pair of melodies shown below in one staff. Distinguish them by keeping the stems consistently up or down, as shown. Add bar-lines to the first melody; then write in the second melody on the same staff. Be sure to align the melodies properly, in that notes sounding simultaneously are to be in vertical alignment.

EXERCISE 14-B: The following groups of three melodies are to be combined in one full score, using treble and bass clefs. The middle melodies are to be added to either the bass or treble clefs according to their staff signs.

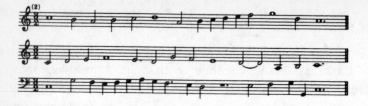

TRIPLETS

Since our notation is essentially binary, it becomes necessary to resort to the use of triplets, as noted before. Thus, an occasional ternary division in the course of a predominantly binary meter will appear as follows:

It is also possible to replace $\frac{12}{8}$ time by $\frac{4}{4}$ time, in which the quarter-notes are subdivided into triplets:

Similarly, $\frac{9}{8}$ time, which might really be better indicated by $\frac{3}{}$., could be replaced by $\frac{3}{4}$ time, using triplet eighth-notes:

DUPLETS

If the meter is primarily ternary, as in $\frac{9}{8}$, and an occasional binary division is desired, duplets will be used, as follows:

RHYTHM

Meter and rhythm are not the same. Meter is always regular, and is abstract. Rhythm is concrete, and may be regular or irregular. We may borrow from poetry some terminology describing certain regular rhythmic patterns, and see how they differ from those of meter.

There are two rhythmic patterns which are especially important for music. The first is called *iambic* rhythm; the basic unit moves from a weak value to a strong value, as in the words *deter, propose*. A poet would refer to each such unit as a *metric foot;* a musician would call each a *rhythmic motif*.

In poetry, such metric feet are combined into lines; thus, we might have lines consisting of only one metric foot (iambic monometer):

Thŭs Ī
Păss by
Ănd die;
Ăs one
Ŭnknown
Ănd gone

—HERRICK, *Upon His Departure Hence*

Or, of two metric feet to the line (iambic dimeter):

Bŭt still thĕ corn
Ăt dawn ŏf morn

Ăt eve lĭes waste
Ă trampled paste

—SCOTT, "Song" from *The Dance of Death*

Also to be found in English poetry are three, four, and more metric feet.

As noted above, the poet refers to these as metric feet; the musician calls them rhythmic motifs (or motives). To use the musical terms, it is possible to have iambic rhythm in both binary and ternary meters, as follows:

The unaccented part of the iambic rhythm is called the *an-*

acrusis; since it occurs on a light beat, it is often called the *up-beat* (coming before a *down-beat,* or accented beat). Notice also that the bar-line is not the natural boundary of the rhythmic pattern; instead, the rhythm flows through the bar-line, which connects the different parts of the rhythm, though it appears to divide it.

Another rhythmic pattern which is important for music is called the *trochaic.* In poetry, trochaic feet follow the pattern which is the reverse of the iambic. The example below is in trochaic pentameter.*

> This of verse alone, one life allows me;
> Verse and nothing else have I to give you.
> —Browning, *One Word More*

Here we have a strong accent followed by a weak syllable. This rhythmic pattern has no up-beat. It is the second basic musical rhythm. These are sometimes called *crusic* rhythms.

SYNCOPATION

The distinction between rhythm and meter enables us to understand what musicians call syncopation. Normally, in music, the rhythm is congruent with the meter, in that the strong beats of the rhythmic patterns coincide with the strong beats of the meter. But where a shift occurs, so that the stresses of the rhythm coincide with the unstressed portions of the meter, then a conflict is set up which we call *syncopation.* Thus, without a regular metric pattern, the concreteness and irregularity

* See Smithberger and McCole, *On Poetry,* New York: Doubleday, Chapter II, for these and other examples of rhythmic patterns.

of rhythm and of rhythmic syncopations could not exist. Below are a few examples of rhythmic syncopations.

III

Introduction to the Scale

THE SIMPLE INTERVALS

An interval, as we learned earlier, is the space framed by two tones of differing pitch. The musical intervals are the simplest harmonic units of music. In fact, it would not be an exaggeration to say that the intervals are the fundamental materials of music; the tones—which we commonly think of as being the materials of music—are, each taken by itself, quite meaningless. Tones acquire musical values insofar as they materialize one or another musical interval.

THE OCTAVE

One of the intervals is, as we have observed, of especial importance. If we start with any tone, and count up (or down) eight tones, we reach another tone having the same name; thus, C–D–E–F–G–A–B–C′; D–E–F–G–A–B–C–D′; and so on. This interval, comprising eight tones, is called the *octave* (from a Latin root meaning eight), and is of fundamental importance for music. The octave unites two tones so closely related that they are given the same name; the tones comprising all other intervals have names different from one another. The sensation given by the octave is that of the same tone reappearing at a higher (or lower) level of pitch. One should note also that although the octave of a tone is the tone most closely related to it, it is also the most remote from it.

All possible tones and tonal relations can be projected within the framework of an octave, and in fact, any complete system of tone relations, when projected into one octave, constitutes what is called a musical *scale*.

WHOLE- AND HALF-STEPS

The piano keyboard is shown below. It will be essential for the student to make constant reference to this diagram in order to understand the materials that follow.

We note that the keyboard consists of a sequence of white and black keys, with the black keys arranged in alternating groups of two and three, which make it possible for the performer to find his way about the keyboard more easily, and that most of the keys have more than one name.

The entire keyboard is divided into *half-steps* (or *semitones*). Thus, a step from any key to its next nearest neighbor is called a half-step. Note that every pair of white keys is separated by a black key, except B–C and E–F.

Two half-steps together make a *whole-step* (or *tone*). Thus, C to C♯ (read C-sharp) is a half-step, and C♯ to D is another half-step. Therefore, C to D is a whole-step. Similarly, D to E♭ (read E-flat) is a half-step, and E♭ to E is another half-step; thus, D to E is a whole-step.

It is essential to remember very clearly that every letter tone is a whole step away from the letter tone on either side of it, *except* B to C, and E to F, which are half-steps. (We will take up the sharps and flats in more detail later on.)

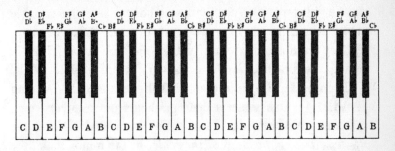

EXERCISE 15-A: Name the keys which are a whole-step above the following keys: C; E; F♯; B; D♭.

(*Note:* The correct name for the tone which is a whole-step above C♯ is D♯. The beginner may ask why it could not be called E♭, inasmuch as the same key may have both names. We follow the rule that the correct name for a tone a whole-step above any letter must be the next letter, and should not skip a letter. Thus, although E♭ could be called a whole-step above C♯, this would skip the letter D. This rule will enable the beginner to avoid mistakes.)

EXERCISE 15-B: Name the keys which are a whole-step *below* the following keys: C; D♭; F; A♭; B♭.

SCALES

We may now approach a definition of the scale. Any octave which is filled in by eight tones may be a scale. The scale may assume a number of forms; that form which is most familiar today is called the *major scale*. This scale runs from C to C'.

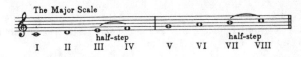

The Major Scale

half-step   half-step
I   II   III   IV   V   VI   VII   VIII

We note the following properties of the scale:* 1) It consists of eight steps. 2) The eighth step has the same letter name as the first; a scale, therefore, consists of seven different tones. 3) Every scale is a mixture of whole- and half-steps. Thus, in the major scale, I–II is a whole-step, as are II–III, IV–V, V–VI, and VI–VII. Note that the half-steps are III–IV, and VII–VIII. 4) One scale is distinguished from another (e.g., the minor scale from the major scale) by *where it places the half-steps among the steps of the scale*. In the minor scale, the half-steps are between steps II–III, and V–VI.

---

* This description applies only to the *diatonic* scale. The chromatic scale is discussed later.

IV

The Major Scale

As noted before, the major scale, like the other diatonic scales, consists of eight steps filling in the octave, and is a mixture of whole- and half-steps. The defining trait of the major scale is that the half-steps are placed between III and IV, and between VII and VIII. If a scale is seen to place the half-steps between any other than these, then it is not a major scale.

The following terms are used interchangeably for the steps of the major scale:

I	Tonic	*Do* (also sometimes *Ut*)	C
II	Supertonic	*Re*	D
III	Mediant	*Mi*	E
IV	Subdominant	*Fa*	F
V	Dominant	*Sol*	G
VI	Submediant	*La*	A
VII	Leading-Tone	*Ti* (also sometimes *Si*)	B
VIII	Tonic	*Do*	C

The beginner must learn to understand these various ways of referring to the steps of the scale: the "solfege" system (*do–re–mi–fa–sol–la–ti–do*) is often to be found in music or books on music printed in French-, Italian-, and Spanish-speaking countries. The letters C–D–E etc., are used in English- and German-speaking countries. The roman numerals, and the terms tonic, supertonic, etc., form the staple terminology of harmony textbooks.

THE INTERVALS OF THE MAJOR SCALE

The major scale gives us the following intervals above the tonic:

1. I–II	C–D	the major second	2	half-steps (or 1 whole-step)
2. I–III	C–E	the major third	4	half-steps (or 2 whole-steps)
3. I–IV	C–F	the perfect fourth	5	half-steps
4. I–V	C–G	the perfect fifth	7	half-steps
5. I–VI	C–A	the major sixth	9	half-steps
6. I–VII	C–B	the major seventh	11	half-steps
7. I–VIII	C–C′	the octave	12	half-steps

| Major 2 | Major 3 | Perf. 4 | Perf. 5 | Major 6 | Major 7 | Octave |

The major scale derives its unique properties of sound from the particular set of intervals—major second, third, sixth, and seventh, etc.—that are built on its tonic.

THE TETRACHORDS

It is common to divide the scale into two halves, each of which is called a *tetrachord* ("group of four tones"). We note that in the major scale the two tetrachords are identical, in that they place the whole- and half-steps in the same order, and we also note that the tetrachords are separated by a whole-step.

TRANSPOSING THE MAJOR SCALE

It is possible to construct the major scale using any tone other than C as the tonic, by an appropriate use of sharps or flats. Every one of the seven basic tones can be raised a half-step if necessary, by means of a sharp sign placed before the note, or it can be lowered a half-step, by means of a flat sign. The *natural* sign (♮), serves to cancel any sharp or flat sign, and restores a note to its natural meaning, as in the scale of C.

If we seek to construct the major scale on any note other than C, we will discover that we must resort to sharps or flats, in order to preserve the proper order of whole- and half-steps as the major scale requires them. If we select the octave from G to G′ for the major scale (that is, we will use G as tonic), we first examine the scale in that octave for its distribution of whole- and half-steps (the student should refer to the diagram of the keyboard):

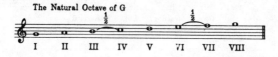

We see that the natural octave from G to G′ does not conform to the pattern of having half-steps between III–IV and VII–VIII; although it does have a half-step between III–IV, it also has the other half-step between VI–VII; VII–VIII (F–G′) is a whole-step. Thus, VII is the "problem" note, too close to VI, too far from VIII. We solve this by substituting F-sharp for F, as the seventh step of the scale. Now we have the major scale on G, with half-steps between III–IV and between VII–VIII, all the other steps being whole-steps:

The G Major Scale

I	Tonic	*Sol*	G
II	Supertonic	*La*	A
III	Mediant	*Ti (Si)*	B
IV	Subdominant	*Do*	C
V	Dominant	*Re*	D
VI	Submediant	*Mi*	E
VII	Leading-Tone	*Fa♯*	F-sharp (F♯)
VIII	Tonic	*Sol*	G

G major requires one sharp, F-sharp.

There is a consistent procedure for constructing all the major scales. Note that, starting with C major, we built the next major key, G major, on the dominant (V) of C; or, another way of putting it, that we started with the upper tetrachord of C major, and used it for the lower tetrachord of the next key (G). For each new scale, the seventh step must be raised.

Upper Tetrachord   Lower Tetrachord
Same as ——————↑

The next major key is built by starting with the dominant of G, or D. Note again that the lower tetrachord places the half-step between III and IV, but the upper tetrachord needs correction, in that the half-step, B–C, is between VI and VII, and that VII to VIII is a whole-step. Again, the seventh step has to be raised. Thus, we substitute C♯ for C, and the upper tetrachord is now congruent with the major scale.

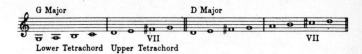

Lower Tetrachord   Upper Tetrachord

By a similar process, the major keys requiring three, four, five, six, and seven sharps, are shown below. (Note that a true fifth above B is *not* F; the true fifth consists of seven, not six, half-steps, and therefore the true fifth above B is F-sharp.)

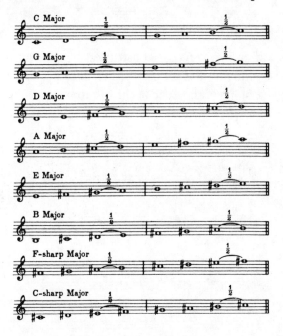

The major keys that require flats can now be constructed. Again we start with C major, but now, rather than transferring the tonic to the dominant, we transfer it to the subdominant (IV). In this case, the upper tetrachord is correct, but the lower is not; although the half-step between VII and VIII is correct, we see that there is a half-step between IV and V, and that III to IV is a whole-step.

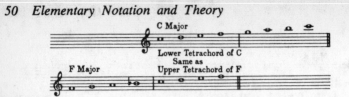

We correct this by lowering, or flatting, the fourth step of the scale. We now have, for F major:

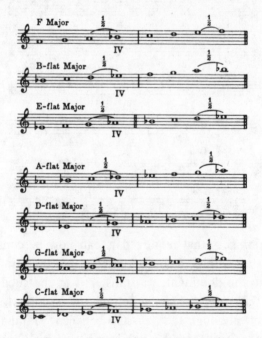

The next flat key, B-flat, is constructed by shifting the tonic to the subdominant, and all the further flat keys are acquired by successive shifts of the tonic to the subdominant:

KEY SIGNATURES

If a musical composition is written in a key requiring sharps or flats, it is not the custom to write a sharp or flat before every note that requires one. Instead, the sharps or flats required for a particular key are collected into a standard pattern which is placed at the beginning of each line of music. This pattern is called the *key signature*. Thus, if a key signature calls for three sharps, F-sharp, C-sharp, and G-sharp (this is A major), the three sharps are placed at the beginning of each line as a reminder to the performer that all and every F, C, and G in the composition is to be sharped, or raised a half-step. Accidentals are added in a consistent pattern.

THE MAJOR KEYS

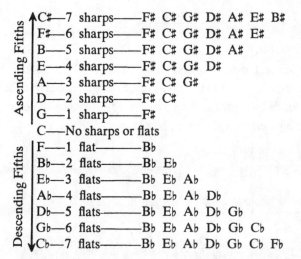

Ascending Fifths		
	C♯—7 sharps	F♯ C♯ G♯ D♯ A♯ E♯ B♯
	F♯—6 sharps	F♯ C♯ G♯ D♯ A♯ E♯
	B—5 sharps	F♯ C♯ G♯ D♯ A♯
	E—4 sharps	F♯ C♯ G♯ D♯
	A—3 sharps	F♯ C♯ G♯
	D—2 sharps	F♯ C♯
	G—1 sharp	F♯
	C—No sharps or flats	
Descending Fifths	F—1 flat	B♭
	B♭—2 flats	B♭ E♭
	E♭—3 flats	B♭ E♭ A♭
	A♭—4 flats	B♭ E♭ A♭ D♭
	D♭—5 flats	B♭ E♭ A♭ D♭ G♭
	G♭—6 flats	B♭ E♭ A♭ D♭ G♭ C♭
	C♭—7 flats	B♭ E♭ A♭ D♭ G♭ C♭ F♭

We see that transferring the tonic upward to the dominant adds a sharp, or subtracts a flat. Also, that flats are subtracted, and

sharps added, by a consistent pattern: the flat to be removed is
a fifth above the last one removed, and the sharp that is to be
added is a fifth above the last one that has been added. Thus,
A major—whose tonic is built on the fifth step of D major—
retains the two sharps of D major, and adds a third, which is
above the last sharp added to give the signature of D major.

We see also that the flat keys are obtained by transferring
the tonic successively downward by fifths, or, which is the
same thing, by transferring the tonic to the fourth step of the
scale, the subdominant. Furthermore, we see that new flats are
added in a consistent pattern, that of retaining the pattern of
flats previously gained, and adding another one, a fifth lower
than the last one added.

Below are all of the major keys, with their key signatures.
Note that although many of these key signatures can be written in more than one way (e.g., the key signature for A major
could appear as this:

or in several other forms), the patterns shown here are, by
convention, almost universally used; departure from these patterns tends to confuse the performing musician, who wishes to
orient himself at a glance as he plays.

ENHARMONIC KEYS

The key signatures shown above number fifteen in all. But the reader who closely examines them and their corresponding keys on the keyboard will realize that three pairs of keys are in a curious relation: C-sharp is the same key on the piano keyboard as D-flat, and so there are two ways of writing the same sound. Accordingly, C-sharp major is identical with D-flat major, note for note. Similarly, F-sharp and G-flat major are identical keys, as are C-flat and B major. Such pairs of keys represent alternate ways of writing the same sounds, and are called *enharmonic* keys (*enharmonic* = "sounding as one").

We have already seen that many notes are enharmonically equivalent—that is, that there are two ways to write a given sound: A-sharp is the same sound, though written differently, as B-flat, and so on; there are only the above three pairs of enharmonic keys in common use.

ENHARMONIC KEYS

C♯ Major—D♭ Major
F♯ Major—G♭ Major
B Major—C♭ Major

DOUBLE SHARPS AND FLATS

The student may wonder if there are not more major keys than these, and may ask if there do not exist keys such as G-sharp major, D-sharp major, A-sharp major, F-flat major, and so on.

There is no reason why such keys could not be used, but in practice they have only a "paper" existence, in theoretical books; composers do not use them. The reason is quite simple: they add no new sounds (G-sharp major is identical in sound with A-flat major; A-sharp major is identical with B-flat major, F-flat with E major; and so on—the student should verify this for himself), and, furthermore, they are extremely difficult to read. F-flat major, for example, would require eight flats. It is much simpler to write it as E major:

F-flat Major (not used) = E Major

It does happen, however, that composers will occasionally venture into such keys, and therefore will require double sharps or double flats. The double flat sign is as follows: ♭♭. The double sharp sign, however, looks like this: ✕

Note that F-double-sharp means F raised by two half-steps, and would be sounded by the key G; B-double-flat means B lowered in pitch by two half-steps, and is sounded by the key A. The student will perhaps see why they are avoided.

ACCIDENTALS

The term *accidentals* is used by musicians sometimes to mean any notes requiring sharps or flats; i.e., any notes other than the seven basic tones, A, B, C, D, E, F, G. Sometimes, however, the term is given a slightly different meaning, referring to any tones which are foreign to a given key. Thus, the notes F-sharp and C-sharp belong to the D-major scale, and so would not be called accidentals, but any notes that do not belong to D major, such as E-flat, F-natural, A-flat, E-sharp, C-natural, etc., would be called accidentals. This second usage is slightly more accurate.

There are a few rules governing the use of these signs:

1. The sharp sign always means, of course, that a given tone is to be raised one half-step in pitch.

2. A flat sign always means that a given tone is to be lowered one half-step in pitch.

3. The natural sign cancels a previous sharp or flat, and therefore sometimes means raising, and sometimes means lowering, the pitch of a note. If F-natural is used to cancel F-sharp, the natural sign has the effect of lowering a tone. If F-natural is meant to cancel F-flat, then it has the effect of raising the tone. The natural sign may itself be understood as producing an accidental, if it introduces a note which does not belong to the scale; thus, E-natural is a note that does not belong to the A-flat major scale, whereas E-flat does, and E-natural, not E-flat, is the accidental.

4. Any sign which is used to introduce an accidental during the course of a piece is considered to be valid for all succeeding notes on the same line or space, until the end of the measure, but after the measure, the key signature again prevails.

EXERCISE 16-A: Label the following notes according to their scale step number (III, I, V, etc.). Label the major key.

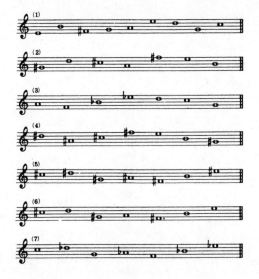

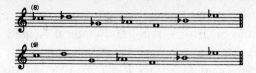

EXERCISE 16-B: Arrange the following key signatures in their conventional order, and indicate the key.

V

The Minor Scale

The minor scale has three forms; we begin with the so-called natural or "pure" minor.

This, like the major scale, has eight steps, and is a mixture of whole- and half-steps. But it differs from the major in its placement of the half-steps. In the major, they are between III–IV and VII–VIII. In the minor, they are found between II–III and V–VI. The minor scale may be found among the white keys of the keyboard by placing the tonic on A:

The minor scale gives us the following intervals above the tonic:

1. I–II	A–B	the major second	2	half-steps
2. I–III	A–C	the minor third	3	half-steps
3. I–IV	A–D	the perfect fourth	5	half-steps
4. I–V	A–E	the perfect fifth	7	half-steps
5. I–VI	A–F	the minor sixth	8	half-steps
6. I–VII	A–G	the minor seventh	10	half-steps
7. I–VIII	A–A′	the octave	12	half-steps

TRANSPOSITIONS OF THE MINOR SCALE

The "natural" key of the minor scale is A minor; it requires no sharps or flats. Like the major scale, it can be transposed to other keys; that is to say, that any note may serve as the tonic of the minor scale. The same pattern of transposition that applied for the major scale also applies for the minor scale: transfer of the tonic to the dominant requires one sharp, F-sharp; transfer to the subdominant requires one flat, B-flat. The entire system of key relations and key signatures seen before applies here as well.

We see from the above that transposing the tonic a fifth upward, to E, requires an adjustment. We have the half-steps between V and VI, where desired, but also between I and II, instead of between II and III. Raising F to F-sharp makes the necessary correction. Similarly, transfer of the tonic to the subdominant, D, gives us the desired half-step between II and III, but also a half-step between VI and VII, where it is not wanted. Lowering B to B-flat places the half-step between V and VI.

The minor scale, unlike the major, has two differing tetrachords; the lower tetrachord has the half-step at the central point of the tetrachord; the upper tetrachord has the half step between the two lowest tones of the tetrachord.

Note that the same key-signature patterns apply for the minor keys as for the major; the key after E minor along the path of ascending fifths is B minor, which requires two sharps,

F-sharp and C-sharp; successive shifts of the tonic by ascending or descending fifths will give us the same patterns of key signatures as before:

THE MINOR KEYS

A♯ minor—7 sharps———	F♯ C♯ G♯ D♯ A♯ E♯ B♯
D♯ minor—6 sharps———	F♯ C♯ G♯ D♯ A♯ E♯
G♯ minor—5 sharps———	F♯ C♯ G♯ D♯ A♯
C♯ minor—4 sharps———	F♯ C♯ G♯ D♯
F♯ minor—3 sharps———	F♯ C♯ G♯
B minor——2 sharps———	F♯ C♯
E minor——1 sharp———	F♯
A minor——No sharps or flats	
D minor——1 flat———	B♭
G minor——2 flats———	B♭ E♭
C minor——3 flats———	B♭ E♭ A♭
F minor——4 flats———	B♭ E♭ A♭ D♭
B♭ minor—5 flats———	B♭ E♭ A♭ D♭ G♭
E♭ minor—6 flats———	B♭ E♭ A♭ D♭ G♭ C♭
A♭ minor—7 flats———	B♭ E♭ A♭ D♭ G♭ C♭ F♭

(Ascending fifths / Descending fifths, marked along the left margin)

Again we see that transferring the tonic upward to the dominant adds a sharp, or subtracts a flat. Also, that flats are subtracted, and sharps added by the same pattern: the flat to be removed is a fifth above the last one removed, and the sharp to be added is a fifth above the last one that has been added.

THE KEY SIGNATURES OF THE MINOR SCALE

Below are the key signatures of the minor scale. The reader will see now that key signatures do not necessarily have one meaning; thus, a key signature of two sharps could mean D major, but it could also mean B minor. It is not possible to tell just by glancing at the key signature what the key or the scale may be; one has to look further. Most melodies begin or end with the tonic note. With practice, one can detect the tonic note even if the melody does not end or begin with the tonic. Once one has both the tonic note and the key signature, one can tell both the key of the piece and the scale. Thus, a key signature of two sharps with a final note of D is D major; the same signature with a final note B is B minor.

Relative Keys   Those major and minor keys which share the same key signatures are called *relative* keys; if a piece of music is written in D major, then B minor is called the *relative minor* of D major; conversely, D major is the *relative major* of B minor.

Parallel Keys   Those major and minor keys which share the same tonics called *parallel keys*. Thus, C minor is the *parallel minor* of C major; E major is the *parallel major of* E minor. (To avoid confusion, or perhaps to compound it, the reader should know that the English-language uses of the terms *relative and parallel* are precisely the opposite of European usage, which leads to difficulty when using music printed abroad; in those books, keys sharing the same tonics are *relative,* and those sharing the same key signatures are *parallel.*)

THE HARMONIC AND MELODIC MINOR SCALES

The minor scale takes two other forms which, however, do not affect the key signatures of the minor scale.

The *harmonic minor* scale is adopted by some composers for harmonic reasons, as the name implies. In the natural or pure minor scale, the seventh step is a whole-step below the eighth. Composers consider certain harmonies to be improved when the seventh step of the minor scale is raised by a half-step, so that there is now a half-step from VII to VIII. The minor scale now has a VII which is, like VII of the major scale, a "leading-tone."

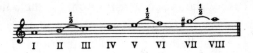

Note that this form of the scale has half-steps between II and III, between V and VI, and between VII and VIII. Furthermore, since VII has been raised by a half-step, the distance between VI and VII is no longer a whole-step, but a step-and-a-half (also called an *augmented second*).

Below are the minor scales, in their "harmonic" form. Note that the key signatures remain the same; since, during the same composition, the seventh step of the scale may sometimes appear in its natural form and at other times may be raised, the raised form is always indicated by an accidental.

The Harmonic Minor Scales

The *melodic minor* scale is derived from the harmonic minor scale. In the latter, the augmented second (the step-and-a-half) between VI and VII is difficult to sing. But if the composer still desires the raised seventh step, the melodic difficulty of the leap between VI and VII may be avoided by raising the sixth step of the scale as well. These alterations of the natural minor normally occur whenever the melody rises from V to VIII; when the melody descends, the scale reverts to the natural form. Below are the minor scales in the form of melodic minor. Again, the key signatures are the same as in the natural minor, as the departures from the natural minor do not always occur in a composition, and are treated as accidentals when they do occur.

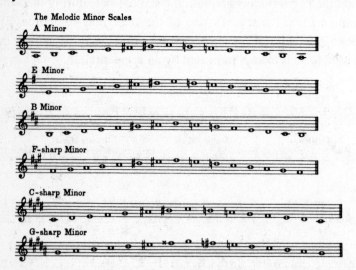

EXERCISE 17: For each of the following groups of notes, determine a) the tonic; b) the scale; whether natural, melodic, or harmonic. State the key.

VI

The Modes

Music possesses a family of diatonic scales, which in earlier times were called *modes*. In the era of modern music, since about 1750, two of these modes became especially prominent; we know them as the major and minor scales. The others became temporarily eclipsed in importance, but today there is a significant revival of compositions written in the modal style. They are indispensable for the music student today.

THE DORIAN MODE

This scale runs in the natural octave from D to D′. It places the half-steps between II and III, and between VI and VII. Both its tetrachords are identical, placing the half-step at the center of the tetrachord.

The Dorian scale gives us the following intervals above the tonic:

1.	I–II	D–E	major second	2	half-steps
2.	I–III	D–F	minor third	3	half-steps
3.	I–IV	D–G	perfect fourth	5	half-steps
4.	I–V	D–A	perfect fifth	7	half-steps
5.	I–VI	D–B	major sixth	9	half-steps
6.	I–VII	D–C	minor seventh	10	half-steps
7.	I–VIII	D–D′	octave	12	half-steps

TRANSPOSITIONS OF THE DORIAN SCALE

Below is the transposition scheme for establishing the tonic of the Dorian mode on any step of the scale. Those with many sharps or flats have rarely been used, but are theoretically quite possible. Note that the same rule applies, that of transferring the tonic successively by ascending and descending fifths, and that the same pattern of key signatures is used.

THE DORIAN SCALE (MODE)

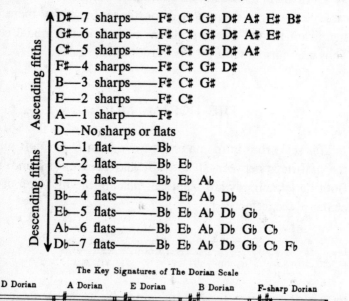

The Key Signatures of The Dorian Scale

D Dorian   G Dorian   C Dorian   F Dorian   B-flat Dorian   etc.

Some Dorian Scales

THE PHRYGIAN MODE

This scale occurs in the natural notes from E to E′; it places the half-steps between I and II, and between V and VI.

The Phrygian Mode

½ step   ½ step

I   II   III   IV   V   VI   VII   VIII

It has available the following intervals above the tonic:

1. I–II	E–F	minor second	1	half-step (or semitone)
2. I–III	E–G	minor third	3	half-steps (3 semitones)
3. I–IV	E–A	perfect fourth	5	half-steps
4. I–V	E–B	perfect fifth	7	half-steps
5. I–VI	E–C	minor sixth	8	half-steps
6. I–VII	E–D	minor seventh	10	half-steps
7. I–VIII	E–E′	octave	12	half-steps

The Phrygian scale follows precisely the same transposition scheme as do all the others; its keys are shown below.

The Key Signatures of The Phrygian Scale

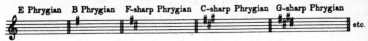

E Phrygian   B Phrygian   F-sharp Phrygian   C-sharp Phrygian   G-sharp Phrygian   etc.

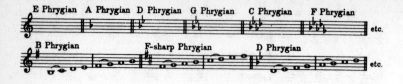

THE LYDIAN MODE

This scale runs from F to F′; it places the half-steps between IV and V, and between VII and VIII. It introduces one interval we have not seen before, between I and IV: the *augmented fourth,* which is six half-steps above the tonic. In all other respects it is identical to the major scale.

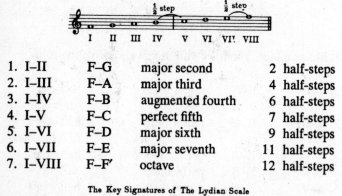

1. I–II   F–G   major second   2 half-steps
2. I–III   F–A   major third   4 half-steps
3. I–IV   F–B   augmented fourth 6 half-steps
4. I–V   F–C   perfect fifth   7 half-steps
5. I–VI   F–D   major sixth   9 half-steps
6. I–VII   F–E   major seventh   11 half-steps
7. I–VIII   F–F′   octave   12 half-steps

THE MIXOLYDIAN MODE

This scale is found in the natural octave from G to G'. It places the half-steps between III and IV, and between VI and VII. Its intervals are identical with those of the major scale, except for its having a minor seventh instead of a major seventh.

1.	I–II	G–A	major second	2 half-steps
2.	I–III	G–B	major third	4 half-steps
3.	I–IV	G–C	perfect fourth	5 half-steps
4.	I–V	G–D	perfect fifth	7 half-steps
5.	I–VI	G–E	major sixth	9 half-steps
6.	I–VII	G–F	minor seventh	10 half-steps
7.	I–VIII	G–G'	octave	12 half-steps

THE IONIAN MODE; THE AEOLIAN MODE

The *Ionian mode* is the scale running from C to C', and is identical with the major scale. The *Aeolian mode* is the natural octave running from A to A', and is identical with the modern minor scale, in its "pure" or natural form.

THE SCALE WITH B AS TONIC

This scale places the half-steps between I and II, and between IV and V. It introduces an interval we have not seen before, from B to F: the diminished fifth, consisting of six half-steps. Because this scale does not have a perfect fifth above the tonic, it has never been used. Some writers refer to it as the *Locrian mode*.

SCALES, KEYS, MODES

It is now evident that a performer can tell nothing about the character of a composition just by examining the array of sharps or flats at the beginning of each staff. A key signature of three flats may mean E-flat major, C minor, F Dorian, G Phrygian, and so on. One must know, in addition to the key signature, the type of scale involved, which in turn means knowing where the half-steps are placed among the eight steps of the scale. The reader must know this with reasonable facility in order to perform or understand a composition.

We may now be able to establish, some slightly clearer terminology with respect to scales, modes, and keys.

The scale, in its generic sense, might be used to mean the entire system of diatonic notes. It consists of a family of *modes* —the Dorian, Phrygian, etc. A mode is one particular form of the diatonic scale, which, by choice of a tonic, places the half-steps in a characteristic and unique way among the eight steps. Every mode is a unique set of musical sounds (*intervals*). A mode may be constructed with its tonic on any particular tone; except for its natural octave, it will need a specific pattern of sharps or flats to present its unique arrangement of whole- and half-steps. In this specific form, we may speak of the key. Thus, the minor mode (or scale) places the half-steps between II and III, and between V and VI, and may be in the key of a minor —C minor, D minor, etc. Thus, for any given composition, we need to know three things: the key signature, the tonic, and the mode.

The exercises following should make this clear.

EXERCISE 18-A: Given the modes below, indicate each mode and its key.

EXERCISE 18-B: Construct the following modes in the keys required below.

1) Phrygian: D-sharp; B; G
2) Dorian: C-sharp; G-sharp; F
3) Lydian: E-flat; D-flat
4) Mixolydian: A-flat; E

THE NAMING OF THE MODES

The modes—Ionian, Dorian, Phrygian, etc.,—were given

these names by medieval musicians, who named them after the Greek tribes, according to the preference of the tribe for a particular mode. It has been since discovered that they relied on erroneous documents, and so mixed up the appropriate names. But the custom survives, and the scales are called the ecclesiastical or church modes, rather than the Greek modes.

VII

The Chromatic Scale and the Intervals

THE CHROMATIC SCALE

Strictly speaking, there is no such thing as a chromatic scale in the sense that there is a diatonic scale. It simply means the collection of all the twelve different tones that fill in the octave. They are normally written with reference to one of the major or minor keys. Since many composers are given to writing in a chromatic style, it may be helpful to show how the complete set of half-steps (the so-called chromatic scale) is written with respect to various keys.

As the scale ascends, the accidentals are usually written in the sharp form; as it descends, they are usually written in the flat form. In some instances, the natural sign will have the effect of raising, and in others, of lowering, a given tone.

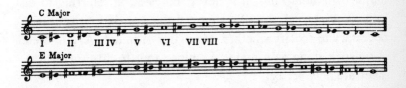

A-flat Major

THE DIATONIC AND CHROMATIC INTERVALS

Knowledge of all the scales and modes now makes it possible to study the musical intervals in their entirety. Their meaning on paper may appear somewhat abstract, but as properties of musical sound they have varying qualities and significance.

Those intervals which occur naturally within the notes of a scale are commonly called *diatonic;* those which occur by chromatic alterations of tones (raising or lowering tones halfsteps, thereby introducing notes that are foreign to the scale), are called *chromatic* intervals.

THE PERFECT INTERVALS
These are the fourth (five half-steps), the fifth (seven halfsteps), and the octave (twelve half-steps).

THE IMPERFECT INTERVALS
These are called "imperfect" because they, unlike the perfect intervals, have a dual character: major-minor. They are the second, third, sixth, and seventh, each of which may be major or minor. Thus, it is never sufficient, in referring to an imperfect interval, to call it simply a third or sixth; it is usually necessary to specify whether it is major or minor. Again, there is no such thing as a major or minor fourth, fifth, or octave. They are only perfect.

The minor intervals are a half-step narrower than their corresponding major forms. Thus the tones forming a minor second are a half-step apart; those forming a major second are a whole-step apart. The tones forming the minor and major third are, respectively, three and four half-steps apart. Thus, C to E-flat is a minor third; C to E (natural) is a major third.

THE CHROMATIC INTERVALS

These normally do not occur within the diatonic scale; they are usually obtained by chromatic alterations.

Below are those chromatic intervals commonly used.

1) *The augmented second.* This is one half-step wider than a major second, and consists of three half-steps (e.g., C to D#). The beginner may ask how the augmented second differs from the minor third (e.g., C to E-flat), since the same key of the piano serves for both E-flat and D-sharp. The answer is that, although the isolated sound is the same, the differing harmonic and melodic contexts within which the intervals are placed serve to give them a different character; by analogy, those English words which have the same sounds but different meanings cannot be spelled interchangeably.

2) *The augmented fourth.* This is one half-step wider than the perfect fourth, and consists of six half-steps.

3) *The diminished fifth.* This is one half-step narrower than the perfect fifth, and consists of six half-steps.

4) *The augmented fifth.* This is one half-step wider than the perfect fifth, and consists of eight half-steps.

5) *The augmented sixth.* This is one half-step wider than the major sixth, and consists of ten half-steps.

6) *The diminished seventh*. This is one half-step narrower than a minor seventh, and consists of nine half-steps.

Note that intervals may be altered by changing the lower tones instead of, or as well as, the upper tones.

We may now collect all the intervals that are in common use, and compare them. We note that in order to construct an augmented interval from one of the imperfect intervals, we must start with the interval in its major form: augmenting (or widening by a half-step) a minor interval will simply produce the interval in its major form. Similarly, an imperfect interval must start with its minor form in order to be diminished.

The reader may ask why other intervals are not mentioned, such as diminished and augmented thirds, a diminished fourth or sixth, an augmented seventh, and a diminished or augmented octave and unison. They are not used because composers have found no meaningful harmonic use for them. The diminished fourth, for example, is identical in sound with a major third, and offers no new resource for the composer; therefore it has only a "paper" existence; no one ever uses it. Although the augmented sixth, for example, is identical in sound with the minor seventh, composers have been able to use it for harmonies other than that involving the minor seventh, and so it has come into use.

The reader now has two tasks to perform. First, he should learn to construct any interval on any given tone. And, conversely, he must learn to recognize any given interval. Exercises are shown below. Some useful hints may be given. If the student is asked to construct a diminished fifth above G, he may begin as follows. He will recall that the diminished fifth consists of six half-steps, and he may then count along the keys of the keyboard as follows: G to G-sharp is one half-step, to A is two, A-sharp three, B is four, C is five, and C-sharp is six. Thus, he may write G to C-sharp as a diminished fifth. But though he has found the right key he has used the wrong name; it should be labeled G to D-flat. Perhaps the best guide for practical purposes is to state that a diminished fifth can only occur between those letter pairs that are fifths apart: C–G, D–A, E–B, F–C, G–D, A–E, B–F, whereas the letter pair G–C, being a fourth apart, will always be a fourth no matter what chromatic alterations are used to produce perfect, augmented, or diminished fourths.

EXERCISE 19-A: Constructing intervals on various tones; construct the required intervals over tones as given below.

1) Augmented fourths, fifths, sixths, and sevenths, on: D-flat; E-flat; G

2) Diminished fifths and sevenths, on: E; F; A

EXERCISE 19-B: Label the intervals shown below. Indicate the complete names, using the abbreviations shown below.

Perfect fourth—Perf 4
Major third—Maj 3
Minor third—Min 3
Augmented sixth—Aug 6
Diminished fifth—Dim 5
etc.

THE TRITONE

The tones B and F stand in a special relation to one another, which is commonly called the *tritone*.

The Tritone as Diminished Fifth   If we take B as the lower tone, we have B to F as a fifth. All the fifths of the natural tones: C–G, D–A, E–B, F–C, G–D, and A–E, are perfect fifths, having seven half-steps. But B–F has only six half-steps. Thus, to construct a perfect fifth above B, F-sharp is necessary. Conversely, to construct a perfect fifth below F, B-flat is necessary.

The Tritone as Augmented Fourth   If F is taken as the lower tone, we see that F to B is an augmented fourth. All the other natural fourths: C–F, D–G, E–A, G–C, A–D, and B–E, are perfect fourths, having five half-steps, while F to B has six. Therefore, to have a perfect fourth above F, B-flat is required, and to have a perfect fourth below B, F-sharp is required.

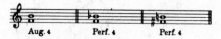

This interval, B–F or F–B, is called the tritone because it may be seen as consisting of three whole-steps: F–G–A–B, or B–C♯–D♯–E♯.

It is this interval which necessitates the chain of successive sharps or flats by ascending or descending fifths in the family of key signatures.

THE INVERSIONS OF INTERVALS

In the example below, we see a short piece consisting of two melodic parts, and in the example following it, we see that the two melodies have been inverted, in that the melody that was lower in the first example is higher in the second. This is commonly called *invertible counterpoint*, and the technique of inverting melodies, harmonies, and intervals is a commonplace of musical practice.

Intervals, when inverted, reveal a series of consistent patterns, as shown below:

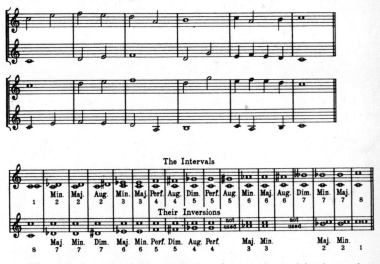

1) The number of an interval plus the number of its inversion always adds up to the sum 9.
2) A major interval when inverted becomes a minor interval.
3) A minor interval when inverted becomes a major interval.
4) An augmented interval becomes diminished when inverted.

5) A diminished interval becomes augmented when inverted.

6) A perfect interval remains perfect when inverted.

VIII

The C-Clefs and Other Clefs

The treble and bass clefs, though more familiar than the others, are not the only clefs in use. Below is the C-clef, which may be used to place Middle C on any line of the staff:

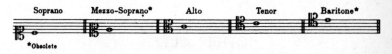

*Obsolete

Of these, the alto, tenor, and soprano clefs should be learned; the mezzo-soprano is also useful for learning to transpose, but is used more rarely.

EXERCISE 20-A: Melodies in the C-clefs. Write the melodies below in alto, tenor, and soprano clefs.

EXERCISE 20-B: Write the following melodies an octave lower, in alto, tenor, and soprano clefs.

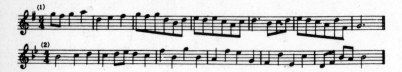

EXERCISE 20-C: Rewrite the following four-part composition in four separate staves, using the soprano, alto, tenor, and bass clefs.

OTHER CLEFS

The student may wish to know of the existence of other clefs, shown below. In the first example, the same melody is shown both in the treble clef and in the French-violin clef. In the second, the same melody is shown in bass clef, sub-bass clef, and in the baritone clef. Note that the baritone clef may also be shown as a C-clef. These clefs are obsolete; of them, the baritone clef is worth learning for the student who may wish to transpose melodies (see Chapter IX, on transposition).

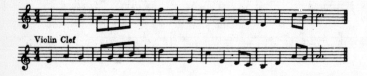

Violin Clef

THE MODERN TENOR CLEF

One other clef deserves mention, as it is commonly used to-day, especially in vocal scores for the tenor voice, in place of the older C-clef. This is the treble clef, which is sung or played an octave lower than written. It commonly appears as below, but also sometimes simply as an unmarked treble clef (the labeling of the part for tenor voice makes it understood that it is performed an octave lower than written):

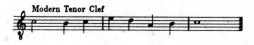

IX

Transposition; Transposing Instruments; Score Reading

One of the more distressing anachronisms of musical notation is the fact that certain musical instruments sound differently than they are written. These are called *transposing* instruments. These make for considerable difficulty in reading orchestral scores.

We may approach the problem in the following terms. Let us imagine a piano which has been mistuned deliberately, so that every string is a whole-step lower than the customary tuning of the piano. If we play the following melody, for example, the actual sounds will be not those written, but as below:

Thus, if we were obliged to use this hypothetical instrument with other musical instruments which are tuned in the customary way, an adjustment of the musical notation would have to be made. In order to get the desired sounds, we would have to write them as:

We would have to write our melody in D major in order to produce a melody in C major. Since, when we play C on this hypothetical piano, we obtain B-flat, we have a "piano in B-flat." Pianos, of course, are not in B-flat, but there are instruments which are, the foremost of which is the clarinet in B-flat. Thus, if a composition is written which includes a clarinet in B-flat, everything for that instrument has to be written a whole-step higher than it actually sounds.

Let us examine the following duet in G major, and arrange it for two instruments—say, violin, and clarinet in B-flat. If we were to arrange it for two violins, the piece could stand as written, as the violin is not a transposing instrument. But the part that is given to the clarinet must be rewritten a whole-step higher, in order to get the sounds desired.

In general, for any instrument in B-flat, that is, any instrument which sounds a whole-step lower than written, the music must be written a whole-step higher. Thus, if the piece is written in F minor, the clarinet part will be written in G minor.

Most of the woodwind instruments of the orchestra are not in C, but some key other than C, which means that they are transposing instruments. Thus, the person wishing to follow a favorite composition with the orchestral score in front of him must be able to comprehend the transposing instruments; in effect this means being able to transpose at sight, or visualize in any key that which has been printed in some other key. Transposition as a notational device was at one time justified because of the technical peculiarities of the wind instruments. But since the nineteenth century, when many technical improvements were made in the wind instruments, these instruments could now be written as they sound. However, this anachronism still survives, and serves only as an impediment to orchestral conductors, as well as to beginners who wish to follow music with score in hand.

Below is a more systematic survey of transposition and the transposing instruments.

TRANSPOSITION

This is the art of performing or visualizing music in any key or at any pitch other than as written. Accompanists and conductors must master this art fully; beginners and those who simply want to follow an orchestral score with comprehension need only learn the most important orchestral transpositions.

There are basically three approaches to transposition:

1) TRANSPOSITION ACCORDING TO THE STEPS OF THE SCALE

In this approach, one simply mentally substitutes the note in the new key which corresponds to the same step-number as in the old key; II for II, III for III, and so on, taking care, of course, to adjust the accidentals that may occur.

Notice, that the accidental sign, when used in transposition, may have three meanings: 1) that a note which is flat in the key is to be raised a half-step; 2) that a note which is sharp in the key is to be lowered by a half-step, or 3) that a note which is an accidental must be restored to its natural value.

EXERCISE 21: Transpose the following melodies into B-flat, D, F, and A, keeping the same clefs.

EXERCISE 22: Arrange the duet on page 86 for violin (the upper voice) and clarinet in B-flat (the lower voice).

2) TRANSPOSITION BY SUBSTITUTION OF CLEFS

The musician who takes the trouble to learn all of the old clefs may use this knowledge as an aid to transposing. He mentally substitutes the appropriate clef sign and key signature, and may thereby visualize the music in the new key. This in some instances requires adjustment by octave transposition.

Thus, the following C major melody may be transposed into any other major key by substitution of clefs and key signatures:

This method of transposition by mentally substituting clefs and key signatures is best left to the advanced student, though the beginner should be aware of it.

3) THE TRANSPOSING INSTRUMENTS OF THE ORCHESTRA

The method of transposing by substituting clefs, while the most thorough, is also the most arduous in terms of the time and effort necessary for learning the old clefs. A short cut to familiarity with the orchestral score is simply that of acquiring facility in reading the most frequently found transpositions in the orchestral score. These follow.

(*a*) *Instruments in B-flat* (clarinet, cornet, trumpet). These sound a whole-step lower than written. In addition, there is the bass clarinet in B-flat, which sounds an octave and a whole-step lower than written.

(*b*) *Instruments in A* (clarinet, cornet, trumpet). These sound a minor third lower than written.

(*c*) *Instruments in F* (Bassett Horn—also called alto clarinet in F—trumpet, horn,* and English horn. The English horn, though not referred to as "in F," uses the same transposition).

(*d*) *Instruments in D* (clarinet, trumpet). These sound a whole-step higher than written.

(*e*) *Instruments in E-flat* (clarinet, alto clarinet, alto saxophone). The clarinet in E-flat sounds a minor third *higher* than written; the alto clarinet in E-flat, and the alto saxophone in E-flat, sound a major sixth *lower* than written.

(*f*) *Octave Transpositions* The piccolo sounds an octave *higher* than written, the double-bassoon and the double-bass, an octave *lower* than written.

EXERCISE 23: Arrange each of the following melodies for the instruments specified, using the appropriate key signature and clef:

Clarinet in B-flat
Horn in F

* Note that the Horn in F (or "French Horn") is never written with a key signature. Instead, every note must have its appropriate sharp, flat, or natural sign. The other instruments, however, do take key signatures.

† Some of these melodies may exceed the actual range of the instruments, but will nevertheless serve the purpose of making the student familiar with the important transpositions.

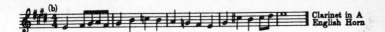

READING AN ORCHESTRAL SCORE

In addition to the C-clefs and the transposing instruments, there is one more peculiarity of the orchestral score which makes for difficulty in its reading. This is that the instruments are not shown in the score according to their range, in the sense that the higher instruments might be placed at the top of the score, with the lower-pitched instruments at the bottom of the score, Instead, the instruments are grouped according to type, as follows:

Woodwinds {
Flutes
Oboes
Clarinets
Bassoons

Brass {
Horns
Trumpets
Trombones
Tubas

Percussion

Harp and/or Piano or Organ

Strings {
Violins
Violas
Violoncellos
Double-Basses

Normally, only those instrumental staves are shown that are being used at a particular point in a score; thus, on one page, when the full orchestra is playing, as many as twenty-four or thirty staves will have to be read simultaneously. At other times, when only a few instruments are being used, as few as two or three staves will be printed. The difficulty for the reader is that this means on occasion the low voices will be printed above those parts sounding higher in pitch, which is harder to visualize, as in the following illustration:

Beethoven, Symphony No. 2 (Finale)

The best exercise for the would-be score reader who finds difficulty in following the score before him is to attempt to reduce a puzzling passage to a simplified piano arrangement.*

EXERCISE 24: Reduce the following brief extract to a piano score. Compare your arrangement with the solution in the appendix. Note that there is no one correct way of doing a reduction; it is an aid to visualizing the orchestral score.

---

* Occasionally, for special effects, a composer may employ *scordatura*, the deliberate mistuning of string instruments such as the violin. When this occurs (e.g., Mahler's *Symphony Number 4*, Mozart's *Sinfonia Concertante in E-flat*, etc.), the string instrument becomes a transposing instrument. Scordatura varies from one work to another. This and a few other peculiarities of orchestral scoring may be explored as they arise, by recourse to such reference works as the *Harvard Dictionary of Music*, Hans Gal's *Directions for Score Reading*, etc.

Beethoven, Pastoral Symphony, Second Movement

X

Performance Markings; Abbreviations; and Miscellany

Performance markings may be described under three headings: *tempo*, or the speed at which the beat moves; *dynamics*, the degree of loudness or softness of performance; and *articulation*, which covers "phrasing"—notes detached from one another or linked together in a manner roughly comparable to varying styles of enunciation of speech. Music being an art of great subjectivity, musicians are greatly at variance as to the meaning of many performance markings.

TEMPO

The only unequivocal way of marking musical tempi is to indicate, by metronome markings, how many beats there should be to the minute (e.g. MM♩ = 60 means 60 quarter-notes to the minute). But no composer ever sets a mathematically exact tempo, or expects a performer to adhere to it. More than one composer's metronome has been known to be inaccurate, so that in any event final recourse must be made to the work itself rather than to metronome markings. The following tempo designations are those commonly used; they are subjective and approximate.

MODERATE TEMPOS

The human pulse of about seventy-two beats to the minute is our normal guide to tempos. Those operating at about seventy-two to the minute, give or take ten beats, are considered moderate:

Andante
Allegro moderato
Tempo giusto
Moderato

FAST TEMPOS

Vivace
Allegro
Presto
Prestissimo

SLOW TEMPOS

Grave
Largo
Lento
Adagio

Some of the above tempo designations are subject to modifications, occasionally with ambiguous results. There are also:

Allegretto, a diminutive of *allegro*. This means fast, but not quite so fast as allegro.

Larghetto, a diminutive of *largo*, means slow but not quite so slow as *largo*.

Adagietto, a diminutive of *adagio*, means *both* the following: 1) slow, but not quite so slow as *adagio;* 2) a piece in the tempo of *adagio,* but shorter than the usual *adagio.*

Andante has undergone an unfortunate development. Originally it meant *moving* (from *andare,* to go), *moderately.* Thus, *più andante* (more *andante*) meant an increase in tempo. But modern musicians have unfortunately taken *andante* to mean slow, so that for modern musicians *più andante,* more *andante,* means a slower tempo. This seems a regrettable barbarism.

Such ambiguity of meaning has spoiled the term *andantino,* which now has three meanings: 1) a piece in the tempo of an *andante,* but shorter than the usual *andante;* 2) "going" or moving, but slower than *andante* (where *andante* is conceived in its earlier meaning); 3) a tempo slightly faster than *andante.* This seems to be the most prevalent meaning today, though usage is not consistent.

It should be emphasized that for the early users of these terms, they referred *not* to the mechanical tempo of a piece, but rather to its style and character; an *adagio* differed from a *largo* in character as much as in tempo. *Allegro* originally meant not "fast," but "cheerful"; *vivace* meant lively, not fast. A *largo* was characterized by an ornate and decorated melodic line, as well as by its slow tempo, a *grave* was mournful, an *adagio* serene.

While regretting the decline of these terms into mere tempo designations, we may now arrange them in a continuous order, on the continuum from very slow to very fast, while being aware of the ambiguities and overlappings that these terms exhibit:

Slow
{
Largo
Lento
Grave
Adagio
}

Moderate
{
Andante
Moderato, tempo moderato
Tempo comodo, tempo ordinario, tempo giusto
Allegretto
Allegro moderato
}

Fast
{
Allegro
Allegro vivace
Vivace
Allegro molto
Presto
}

To these may be added: *larghetto*, slightly faster than *largo*; *adagietto*, slightly faster than *adagio*; *andantino*, slightly slower (sometimes slightly faster) than *andante*; *prestissimo*, faster than *presto*.

DYNAMICS

These terms and markings refer to the force or loudness of performance. Here, too, a change in meaning has occurred; for older musicians, variations in dynamics were as much along the continuum of hardness-and-softness of tone as they were along the scale of decibel rating. Thus, *forte* meant an attack on a note of a more biting and heavy character (admittedly more subjective in meaning), rather than a sharp increase of the mere loudness of the note.

The following terms are in common use, with their abbreviations:

Forte, strong (today: loud) *f*

Fortissimo, very strong (today: very loud) *ff*

Mezzo Forte, moderately loud *mf*

Piano, soft, quiet *p*

Pianissimo, very soft, very quiet *pp*

Mezzo Piano, moderately soft (not as soft as piano) *mp*

Crescendo (cresc), becoming louder, also shown by this sign: <

Decrescendo (decresc), and *diminuendo* (dim), becoming softer; also: >

Forte-Piano: fp suddenly loud, followed by soft

Sforzato, sforzando: sf, sfz like forte-piano, a sudden spasmodic forte, immediately followed by soft

Calando, morendo, perdendosi: becoming gradually slower and softer.

ARTICULATION

These terms refer to manner of performance other than speed or volume. *Staccato notes,* shown by dots, refer to notes that are shortened in value to give the effect of being detached and separate in character:

Mezzo-staccato (semi-detached)

Staccato (shortened somewhat)

Staccatissimo (very short and sharp in character)

Legato notes are very very smoothly linked together with no noticeable discontinuity between one note and the next, as though reminiscent of the tonal continuity of a siren.

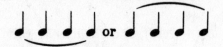

Accents are shown by the following marks:

Mild   **Strong**   **Very Strong**

REPEAT SIGNS

A double bar is used to indicate the end of a section or a piece. The placing of dots indicates repeats, as follows.

(1) The following means that the music *up to* the double bar is to be repeated:

(2) The following means that the music *after* the double bar is to be repeated:

(3) The following shows that the music *both before and after* the double bar is to be repeated (a composition in two sections, each of which is to be repeated):

A composition in the form A–B–A, in which the third section is simply a repetition of the first, is often written out as follows:

or:

D.C. means *Da Capo,* to start again from the beginning ("from the head"). D.S., *Dal Segno,* means repeat from the sign. The end of the piece is marked by the word *Fine* (the end), or by a "hold" sign: ⌢ over the final point of the piece.

FIRST AND SECOND ENDINGS

It is sometimes necessary to alter the ending of a repeated section, at the point where the piece is either to be repeated, or where the repeat has been performed, and the piece is now to go on.

A FEW COMMON SIGNS AND
ABBREVIATIONS

Term	Written	Played

PART TWO

Classroom Exercises in Intervals, Melody, and Rhythm

Preface to Part II

Following are a set of exercises for beginning groups in the classroom. They include single melodies of the *solfege* type, and simple two- and three-part exercises. They seek to cover all of the scales, modes, intervals, and rhythmic patterns that the beginner needs to master. The teacher will notice that many of the exercises follow the character of species-counterpoint writing; the author has confirmed that the singing of simple exercises in species counterpoint is an extremely effective way of learning the fundamentals of music for all beginners. It is recommended that each exercise be rehearsed until it is well-learned, and that the class be divided into groups which take turns singing each part. Thus, for singing a two-part exercise, one-half the class sing the upper voice, the other the lower voice; once it is well-learned, the two groups exchange voices and repeat again until well-learned. If most of these exercises are repeated until practically memorized, the beginner will have acquired a full vocabulary of the basic musical sounds, idioms, and performing problems.

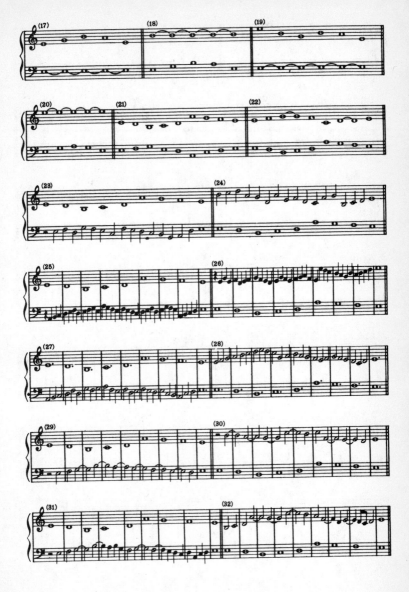

RHYTHM EXERCISES

The following exercises provide a brief introduction to the problem of performing syncopated rhythms; these are patterns in which rhythmic emphasis operates in conflict with the normal emphasis provided by the meter.

APPENDIX

Solutions to Exercises

EXERCISE 1:
No solutions required.

EXERCISE 2:
(a) CFBEDAECABCGDCFC.
(b) CGDEFEAGEFCC′GDGB.
(c) EGBEDGABECFDGEAF.
(d) FDBGEAGFEABCDE.
(e) ADFBG′GBGCEAFGBCD.
(f) AGFBAEBDBGCCDE.
(g) FCBCEBGEAFDEC.

EXERCISE 3:
No solutions required.

EXERCISE 4:
(a) ECGEDFEGFDBCAEGDFG.
(b) GFFEEDDCCBGAEFC.

EXERCISE 5:
EGCDGDB.   DAFBGE.

EXERCISE 6:
No solutions required.

EXERCISE 7:
(a) C G D A E B F C G B F A E G D F G.
(b) G D A E C B G B F C C F B E A D C.
(c) C C B B A A G G F F E E D D C C.
(d) F C G D A E B F C G G C.
(e) C G D D A E E F F G G C.

EXERCISE 8-A:
(1) C B A E F D E B C E A B C.
(2) G F E D F E D C E A G B C.
(3) E B D C B G A F B A G F E.
(4) A E F D E C D B A.

EXERCISE 8-B:
No solutions required.

EXERCISE 9-A:

C B C A B C G A D C

EXERCISE 9-B:

C B D E G A F D C

EXERCISE 9-C:

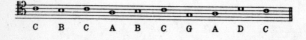

C B C A B C G A D C

EXERCISE 9-D:

C B D E G A F D C

EXERCISE 9-E:

EXERCISE 9-F:

C G A E F F D A B C

EXERCISE 10:

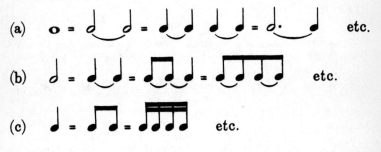

(a)

(b)

(c)

(d)

(e)

EXERCISE 11:

(a)

(b)

(c)

(d)

Exercise 12-A:

Exercise 12-B:

Exercise 12-C:

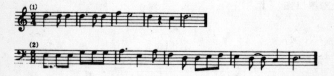

EXERCISE 12-D:

EXERCISE 13-A:

EXERCISE 13-B:

EXERCISE 14-A:

EXERCISE 14-B:

EXERCISE 15-A:

D; F-sharp; G-sharp; C-sharp; E-flat.

EXERCISE 15-B:

B-flat; C-flat; E-flat; G-flat; A-flat.

EXERCISE 16-A:

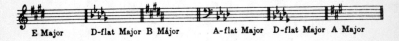

EXERCISE 16-B:

EXERCISE 17:

(a) B-flat minor, natural. (b) E minor, natural. (c) B minor, natural. (d) C minor, natural. (e) E minor, melodic. (f) C minor, melodic.

EXERCISE 18-A:

(1) Mixolydian, A-flat. (2) Phrygian, D. (3) Dorian, F-sharp. (4) Lydian, A-flat. (5) Dorian, B-flat. (6) C-sharp minor, harmonic. (7) Lydian, B.

EXERCISE 18-B:

Exercise 19-A: 1)

Exercise 19-A: 2)

Exercise 19-B:

(1) Aug 5. (2) Perf 5. (3) Dim 5. (4) Min 7. (5) Maj 7. (6) Dim 7. (7) Dim 7. (8) Min 7. (9) Maj 7. (10) Perf 4. (11) Aug 4. (12) Aug 6. (13) Min 6. (14) Maj 2. (15) Aug 4.

Exercise 20-A:

EXERCISE 20-B:

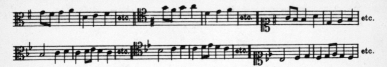

EXERCISE 20-C:

EXERCISE 21:

Solution not required.

EXERCISE 22:

EXERCISE 23:

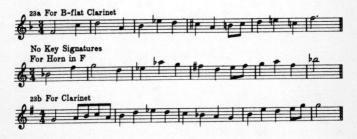

For English Horn

EXERCISE 24: